MARTIN LUTHER KING, JR.

Gloria D. Miklowitz

Publisher: Raymond Yuen
Editor: John S. F. Graham
Designer: Greg DiGenti
Photo Credits: Bettmann/Corbis (cover and pages 6, 15, 21, 26) ; Hulton-Deutsch Collection/Corbis (Page 11)

Published by:

↯ Dominie Press, Inc.
1949 Kellogg Avenue
Carlsbad, California 92008 USA

www.dominie.com

Paperback ISBN 0-7685-1219-0
Library Bound Edition ISBN 0-7685-1544-0
Printed in Singapore by PH Productions Pte Ltd
1 2 3 4 5 6 PH 04 03 02

Table of Contents

Chapter 1

A Pair of Shoes

Martin Luther King, Jr. was born on January 15, 1929, in Atlanta, Georgia.

At that time, it was against the law for blacks to eat in restaurants where white people ate. They could not go to schools with whites or use the same

restrooms or water fountains. They
had to sit in the back of a bus. They
had to sit in different places from
whites in movie theaters and on trains.
Because of Martin Luther King, Jr.,
many laws unfair to black people
were changed. Because of him,
problems of the poor became important
to everyone, and Americans of every

Martin Luther King, Jr. gives a speech
in Cleveland, Ohio for voter rights

color began to understand and accept each other better.

When Martin Luther King, Jr. was a child, his father, a respected minister in Atlanta, took him to buy a pair of shoes. The Reverend King led young Martin to a seat near the front of the store.

"Move to the rear of the store, please," the clerk said. "I'll serve you there. Blacks sit in back or they don't get served!" Martin's father got up, took his hand, and left the store.

As soon as Martin could read, he tried to learn everything he could about slavery and about blacks in the United States. By the time he was 13, he figured that to be successful in a mostly white country, a black man had to be twice as good and twice as smart as everyone else.

He graduated from high school in 1944 at only 15 and went to Morehouse College in Atlanta. Other students partied, but Martin spent many hours reading history and discussing ideas with friends. He wasn't sure what he wanted to be—a doctor, a lawyer, or a preacher, like his father. Finally he decided to be a preacher, but not like other preachers who only helped people escape their worries. He wanted to be able to do more.

Chapter 2

Nonviolence

Martin didn't go home after college. He enrolled at Crozer Seminary in Pennsylvania to study for a master's degree.

Crozer was in the North, where there

were no laws based on race. Martin could sit wherever he wanted in a restaurant or a theater. One day, he heard a lecture about Mohandas K. Gandhi, a leader in India who believed in nonviolence.

Gandhi told his people to free themselves from British rule without ever raising a hand or firing a shot. Gandhi was a very influential leader for protest movements around the world and in the United States because he was successful without being violent. Although Gandhi was jailed often, he never fought back.

Martin was excited by the idea that change could be brought about peacefully, and it became central to his beliefs about creating change in the United States.

*Martin Luther King, Jr. addresses a crowd
at the March on Washington*

In 1951, Martin began work on a
doctoral degree at Boston College. His
small apartment became the meeting
place for black students. They drank
coffee and talked for hours about
how blacks and the poor were treated.
Most white people coming back from

overseas in World War II were treated as heroes, but that wasn't true for blacks. Martin and his friends said that even black heroes of the war were treated as second-class citizens because of the color of their skin.

In Boston, he met Coretta Scott, a pretty young woman from Alabama. She wanted to become a concert singer. She didn't want to return to the South, where her father's business had been burned to the ground because he was black. Nevertheless, when they married, Martin accepted a job in Montgomery, Alabama. He liked the people in the congregation. They wanted, as he did, a church of worship where ideas could be shared.

Shortly before Martin moved to Montgomery, the federal government ruled that separate schools for black and white children were illegal. This law angered many white Southerners who did not want to allow black children into white schools or change the old ways.

Chapter 3

The Back of the Bus

On December 1, 1955, a thin, black seamstress named Rosa Parks boarded a bus to go home. Her back ached and her legs hurt from working and Christmas shopping. She paid her fare in front of the bus, then hurried off the

*Martin Luther King, Jr. sits in a jail cell
in Birmingham, Alabama*

15

bus and ran to the back door where blacks got on. The first four rows were for whites only. She found a seat in the fifth row.

The bus filled quickly, and soon the first four rows were taken. Seeing whites standing, the driver told Rosa to giver her seat to a white person. "No," she said. "I won't!" Because she refused, Rosa Parks was arrested for disobeying race laws.

The news of her arrest spread. Soon a meeting was held at Martin's church. More than 40 important black men and women came. It was time to act, not just talk. They decided all blacks should boycott the buses, not riding them until bus companies showed respect to black passengers.

Posters were printed, reading: "Don't ride the bus to work, to town, to school, or anyplace Monday. Take a cab, share a ride, or walk." On Monday, Martin and his wife, Coretta, waited for the 6:00 a.m. bus, which was usually full of blacks going to work. That morning, it was empty. Blacks walked or thumbed rides. Taxis were full. Some even rode mules to work. Each day of the boycott, the bus companies lost money.

Martin became the leader of this protest. He called on all blacks to unite. What blacks wanted, through peaceful protest, were their civil rights—and they wanted them now.

Chapter 4

Peaceful Protest

Blacks wanted what whites already
enjoyed: to be treated politely by bus
drivers, to sit in any empty seat, and to
drive buses in their own neighborhoods.
City leaders denied these requests.

The boycott went on. Over Christmas, white businesses did poorly because fewer people went into the city to shop.

In the next several weeks and months, blacks shared cabs, car-pooled, but would not ride the buses. City officials, hoping to turn people against Martin, said he drove expensive cars and was power hungry.

Blacks waiting for their carpools were told they'd be arrested for hitchhiking. Carpool drivers were arrested for driving five miles over the speed limit. Someone tried to bomb his house. "We must meet violence with nonviolence," he told a crowd wanting to fight back. "He who lives by the sword shall perish by the sword."

Lawyers said the boycott was illegal

and arrested Martin and other black
leaders. Some of them were sentenced
to jail, while others were fined $500.
Six months later, federal judges ruled
that bus segregation was against the
Constitution. Angry, some whites
bombed black homes and churches.
Just when city officials were going
to outlaw carpools, the Supreme
Court announced that bus segregation
was illegal.

The peaceful protest worked. Almost
a year after the boycott began, Martin
and others went to catch the 6:00 a.m.
bus. Martin boarded and sat where he
pleased. In 1956, the first integrated bus
in the history of the South rolled on
down the street.

Boycotts spread all over the South.
Martin told blacks to peacefully disobey

Martin Luther King, Jr. is arrested by police for loitering in front of a courthouse where a fellow civil rights volunteer was giving testimony

laws refusing them rights that white people enjoyed. In 1957, almost 30,000 black and white Americans marched to Washington, D.C. to protest unfair treatment. There, Martin set the next goal.

Few blacks could vote because Southern states made it so hard to register.

"Give us the vote," Martin said, "and we will write the proper laws."

Chapter 5

Opening Up

Blacks were still segregated in the South. They could not sit with whites in restaurants, libraries, or theaters. Blacks could not drink from the same drinking fountains or go to the same restrooms as white people. To protest this unfairness, black students sat at white lunch counters. They stood and knelt in churches where blacks weren't allowed. They stayed until the police arrested them.

Some buses, going between states, were still segregated. To change this, thirteen white and black students boarded a bus in Washington, D.C. headed south towards New Orleans. They called themselves the "Freedom Riders." Wherever the bus stopped in the South they got out to sit at "whites only" lunch counters and waiting rooms.

In Alabama, a wild mob of whites set fire to the bus. The students boarded another bus to Birmingham, Alabama, where they were attacked and beaten. The violence was so bad that the Federal government sent in hundreds of U.S. Marshals.

More people joined the protesters. Martin decided Birmingham needed "opening up." He arranged a march on City Hall. The police ordered the marchers to stop. They wouldn't stop but didn't resist when the police arrested them. Even Martin was arrested. He was jailed 30 times in his life.

Even more people joined the protesters, white people as well as black people. Police used high-powered water hoses, clubs, and attack dogs against them. On one day, almost 1,000 people were put into jails that couldn't handle that many. Losing money, white businesses agreed to the freedom movement's demands.

Martin arranged a peaceful march to the Lincoln Memorial in Washington. On August 28, 1963, more than 200,000

Martin Luther King, Jr. with civil rights
marchers in Montgomery, Alabama

Americans came to sing freedom songs
and hear speeches. Martin said, "I have
a dream, that all God's children... will
be able to hold hands." Despite the
gains, violence against the protesters
continued.

In 1964, Congress passed the Civil
Rights Act. It called for desegregation
of all public places. Refusing to hire

someone or let someone vote because of his or her color became illegal.

Martin received many honors for his work. He was named Man of the Year by *Time* magazine. Yale University awarded him an honorary degree for refusing to use violence. And he won the Nobel Peace Prize.

But some whites were unhappy with him for bringing change. They believed that black people were somehow inferior to whites and shouldn't be given the same rights. Martin was threatened many times by people who wanted him to stop. In 1968, he was assassinated, killed by a gunman's bullet. He was only 39 years old.

Having patience and the love of all of humanity, Martin Luther King, Jr.

is remembered as the man who helped change the world for the better. Because of him, we now have laws that make it illegal to discriminate against people based on their skin color or where they came from.

In 1983, president Ronald Reagan signed a law that made Martin Luther King Jr.'s birthday a national holiday.

Glossary

Atlanta - the capital of Georgia.

Assassinated - when a public figure or government official is killed by someone for political reasons.

Birmingham - a large city in Alabama

Boycott - an organized movement to stop buying from a company or government in order to protest against its policies.

The Constitution - the legal document that contains the rules and laws that the United States government follows.

Desegregation - a political movement to end separate rules for black people and white people. see *Segregation*

Discriminate - to treat a group of people differently—often worse—than other groups of people.

Doctoral Degree - the highest college degree someone can achieve. Also called a *doctorate*.

Enrolled - when someone is going to school.

Federal - having to do with the United States government.

Gandhi - one of the most respected leaders of the 20th century. He said that people could protest unfair laws and policies by peaceful protest, without using violence.

Hitchhiking - traveling by taking car rides with strangers. This was much more common and safer in the 1950s and 1960s than it is today. see *Thumbed*

Honorary Degree - a degree given by universities

and colleges to someone who has accomplished something great, even though they haven't attended or finished the required schoolwork.

Influential - having an effect on other people.

Integrated - when two or more groups are together.

Lecture - a speech given by a professor on a topic in class.

Lunch Counters - in the 1940s and 1950s, some stores, like drugstores and department stores, had small restaurants in them where people sat at a counter in front of the kitchen.

Montgomery - the capital of Alabama.

Negro - a term used in the early and mid-20th century to refer to black people. This term is not used very much anymore.

Nevertheless - in spite of.

Nobel Prize - an award given to someone who has contributed to world culture either scientifically or socially.

Preacher - a religious leader who gives speeches.

Seamstress - someone who sews or works with material to make clothing.

Segregation - a political movement that kept people of different skin colors from going to the same places or receiving the same types of services.

Seminary - a religious type of college.

Supreme Court - the most powerful legal group in the United States. It is made up of nine judges and is one of the three branches of the United States government. The other two are Congress and the President.

Thumbed - to "thumb a ride" means "to hitchhike." People along the side of a road would put their thumbs out to show which direction they wanted to go. Then a car would stop for them and take them for a ride in that direction.

U.S. Marshals - a kind of police force to protect people in the legal system in the United States.

Yale - a university in Connecticut; it is part of the "Ivy League."